Table of Contents

Dedication 4

Acknowledgment 5

Foreword 8

Introduction 10

Chaper One: Push Forward 12

Chapter Two: Get your credit up and your debt down ... 20

Chapter Three: Second Chances 25

Chapter Four: Letting Go of Church Hurt 33

Chapter Five: Processing Grief 41

Chapter Six: Breaking Generational Curses 47

Chapter Seven: Release Every Weight 57

Chapter Eight: Leave a Legacy 63

Dedication

I dedicate this book to my beautiful, wisdom-filled mother, Deborah Anderson, My step-father, Willie Anderson, and my baby brother, Trumaine Anderson. Your love and guidance will forever live on.

Acknowledgment

I am humbly grateful to God for His divine guidance, strength, and inspiration that have illuminated my life's path and fueled the creation of this book. Without Your divine presence, I cannot fathom where I would be today.

I want to express my deepest gratitude to my husband for his unwavering support and encouragement throughout this journey, not only with this book but also in my evolution as a woman. Through our relationship's many ebbs and flows, after 20-plus years, we still wake up daily and choose us. I love you forever.

To my beloved father, Mr. Fredel Wilson, your resolute commitment to putting God first through your devout prayers and active involvement in the church, your selfless dedication to our family and community, and your boundless generosity have been priceless treasures that continue to shape my adult life. I will forever cherish being a Daddy's Girl.

To my three beloved children, my ultimate motivation and inspiration, I extend my deepest love and gratitude for your patience and understanding as I dedicated myself to my career, personal growth, and development.

Every effort was made with the sole purpose of securing a brighter future for you.

My dearest siblings, life wouldn't have been as exciting and adventurous without you guys, and I don't believe they create siblings as tight as we were anymore, so we must always count our blessings and memories.

From Brokenness to Wholeness

A Journey to Healing from Trauma, Grief and Loss

Foreword

If you are a woman and find yourself broken and stuck spiritually, emotionally, physically, vocationally, and financially, then this book is for you!

From Brokenness to Wholeness: A Journey to Healing from Trauma, grief, and Loss can be read from cover to cover in one or two sittings, but the wisdom, advice, and counsel found within its pages will last a lifetime.

Kasha Haywood has taken the devastating experiences in her life—surviving abuse of many forms (physical, mental, sexual), poverty, divorce, and much more—and shown how God intervened and transformed her life into one that is happy, WHOLE, and abundantly blessed. Kasha no longer suffers from the negative effects of what she experienced but now uses her voice and testimony to coach and guide other women out of similar circumstances.

As a professional licensed mental health counselor in the behavioral health industry, I've counseled clients from all walks of life and can attest to the deep and debilitating effects of trauma and many other mental health issues highlighted in this book. It is only through casting your faith in God AND doing the necessary work that you will see lasting and sustaining results. Kasha has showcased that within the pages of this book.

I highly recommend From Brokenness to Wholeness: A Journey to Healing from Trauma, grief, and Loss. This book should be placed in every woman's shelter, drug and alcohol facility, prison cells, hospital emergency rooms, church libraries, and anywhere broken women can be found.

Congratulations on this great work that will help so many people, Kasha!

Sarah A. James, MS, LMHC
Chayil Christian Counseling Services

Introduction

In October 2020, God awakened me from sleeping and had me write down The WHOLE Woman Concept. It was such a powerful revelation that I established an LLC without knowing what it meant or what he wanted me to do with it. Over time, God started revealing more details to me, some of which are included as topics in this book. Initially, I questioned why God would have me revisit these painful life experiences. I had buried many of them because they no longer defined me, and I couldn't resonate with them anymore. That's when God instructed me to start writing this book. Then I questioned why God would give me such a responsibility to impart this to his creation of women. As I asked this question, it began to unfold. As far back as I can remember, Satan has been trying to kill me. From childhood trauma, molestation, teen pregnancy, domestic violence, divorce, insecurity, self-hate, suicide ideation, obesity, debt, church hurt, betrayal by friends, and the loss of loved ones. I've experienced inconceivable pains in brokenness, but God healed me from them all. He made me WHOLE!

> *And He said unto her, "Daughter, thy faith hath made thee whole; go in peace, and be whole of thy plague."* (**Mark 5:34**)

Chaper One

Push Forward

I used to say I don't like weak women. Sometimes, I still catch myself saying it, especially when I see women put their children in harm's way and toxic environments for the temporary comfort of a man's validation and warm bed. But I've come to understand that not everyone can handle tough situations the same way. We come from different cultures, backgrounds, and upbringings, and some women need more time and support to leave bad situations. It's not always easy to exit once your soul is fractured, but that's when you look to your kids and lean on them as your strength and motivation to do what's right.

Following my divorce from my ex-husband, not much changed except for the fact that I inherited debt. I was already used to facing challenges; that was one of the minor reasons for my decision to leave. I say minor because there were more pressing issues at hand in our relationship. I endured years of physical and emotional abuse. He would also destroy my property. It reached a point where one day I'd wake up to a shattered car windshield, only to find myself in the emergency room the next day, dealing with a fractured wrist from one of his rageful attacks. He would slap, kick, punch, spit in my face, and beat me like I was a man. He would say such hurtful things to me that, at times, I found myself wishing he would physically hit me instead because the pain from his words lasted far longer than any physical blow. By now, you're probably wondering why I stayed. Part of me held onto the hope that the person I fell in love with would resurface—the one who showed me love, kindness, and tender affection. I suppose you could say I was still chasing that feeling—the person who once promised me the world, and I saw him pursuing it at times. Truthfully, I was also very young and naive. So, during my healing journey after my divorce, I had to learn to give myself grace from that younger perspective. My frontal lobes weren't fully developed; truthfully, neither were his. The frontal lobes are the brain parts responsible for learning, emotions, impulse control, and problem-solving. However, it doesn't excuse knowing right from wrong and refraining from hurting others.

It wasn't until the day he had me in a chokehold, my life slipping away as I begged for mercy, that everything changed. The last image I saw was my 8-month-old baby standing in her crib, crying. I don't know what made him release me, but I survived, and in that moment, I knew I was done. I made a vow to myself—I wouldn't let my daughters grow up believing this was love. I refuse to allow them to think it's acceptable for a man to abuse them physically. My throat was bruised and sore for a month after that incident, but my heart, which used to be soft and hurt, became solid and hard. I knew no man would ever hurt me again, starting with him. With no money, leaving wasn't an option, and I was too embarrassed to let family and friends know what was going on, so I endured it all in silence. I had never fought him back, but he meant nothing to me at this point. The next time he tried to hit me, I snapped. I fought back so hard that even he was taken aback. I felt accomplished as he acted like a victim. I remember telling him, "I learned from the best, didn't I? You taught me well."

I ended up confiding in my best friend, who swore me to secrecy, but as soon as I hung up the phone, she called my mother. Can you believe I stopped talking to her for sharing something that could've cost me my life? She only told my mom because she was afraid for my life. I couldn't see that at the time because the thinking of abused people is often distorted. They may turn on you for trying to help them. I eventually devised a solid plan to leave, but not before my mom flew to Illinois and took her grandkids. She said, and I quote verbatim. "He ain't shit, and you ain't gone ever have shit as long as you stay with him, but my grandkids will not be caught up in this," and she left with my babies. She was saying I would never have anything because he had broken up many of the new things she had purchased for us to move into our new apartment. My mom's words and delivery were raw, but she was always right, and deep down, I knew it. Her words gave me the extra push I needed to get things moving.

I knew I could handle the struggle alone; I'd been doing it already. There was no chance I'd let myself and my kids endure pain and hardship just to say I had a man. That's just dumb. With about $900 in my savings account, I took $700 and hired a lawyer to file for divorce. The divorce was painful and drawn out too, but I'll spare you those details. However, in the finalized divorce decree, he was ordered to pay me $350 a month for child support for two kids. That amount didn't even cover my daycare bill. However, that didn't matter because I never received that court-ordered money from him anyway. In 18 years, he only gave me $50 once. Yes, it hurt because I felt betrayed, and I struggled, and life just wasn't fair to me. But I didn't have time to cry, chase him, or worry about what he might be doing with another woman and her kids. Women waste too much time fretting over those matters that don't concern them, when they could be focusing on leveling up during this time.

My mindset was simple: I had to do whatever needed to be done for myself and my children. I had more mouths to feed than food in the fridge and more bills than money. I couldn't tell the electric company that I was waiting on child support owed to me, so I couldn't pay them. I can assure you they wouldn't care. I also couldn't share my sob story with the daycare center. If my kids lost their spots there, how was I going to report to duty? So, daycare is just as important as rent for military members. I had to make a lot of sacrifices for my kids. There was no getting my hair and nails done, wearing the latest trends, or eating out. I couldn't get food stamps because they said I made too much, and I didn't have someone like me (today) around whom I could readily call and ask for money. Those I did ask claimed never to have it or made me feel so guilty that I decided never to ask again. Because of this, I learned to be self-sufficient and have never asked anyone for money since I was 21.

That means I had to sacrifice a lot of my wants and needs. So, chasing this man or any man was out of the question. Not to mention, I didn't have the time or money to take my ex back to court, so it was what it was. I started focusing on getting promoted. One of my friends, who had lots of experience using the military tuition assistance program, helped me enroll, and I started taking college courses. She would even babysit my kids while I attended class. The Air Force is big on education—it's essential for career progression. I needed my education regardless because I wasn't sure if I would stay in the military or leave, and I needed something to fall back on if I decided to leave.

I see too many women getting caught up in the pursuit of what's owed to them and searching for someone to take care of them, neglecting to focus on bettering themselves. I remember the feeling of wondering why he gets to enjoy his life while I'm stuck here, suffering. It's a genuine feeling, and it's completely validated. By all means, if you have the time and resources for the chase, then go for it. But this advice is for those who don't have it like that. I've seen people become bitter over these situations, constantly worrying about him and his new life with someone else. For years, I've heard the same stories, and all the while, no progress has been made in the woman's own life. It's crucial to create goals and stay focused on them.

I never became bitter, and I never spoke ill of him. Please don't be one of those women who speak badly of the other parent to the kids. Until this day, I haven't spoken ill of him to the kids or anyone else. What I did do was forgive myself and forgive him, and I Bossed Up! Anything he would've given to me would have only been extra because it was no longer needed for the survival of my household. And that's how I want it for every woman. As you're focusing on yourself with self-development, personal development, and spiritual growth, at the right time, God will send the right man your way. Yes, you can still get a great partner after a divorce, even if you have kids. Please don't believe the lies of society or that jealous friend or mean ex, because they couldn't serve you properly. To be fair to this new partner, present a new and improved version of yourself. Don't be a broken project for them to fix. No one deserves that, not even you, for coming with some extra baggage. I've been married to a wonderful man for over 20 years.

Words of advice:

1. Watch your daughters. I was just a teenager when the abuse started for me, and I equated it to love. Teach your daughters to love themselves and what right love looks and feels like. Their father or fatherlike figure would be a great teacher of this.

2. If you're being abused, please don't allow it to linger because it can cost you your life. Remember, no one will take care of your babies like you if you're not around. You don't deserve any type of abuse, even if he tries to make you believe it's your fault. Tell someone you can trust and leave immediately. There are shelters and safe havens where you can go with your kids.

3. Don't repeat history. Learn yourself inside and out. Figure out how you ended up in this situation and never allow it to happen again. Create life values for yourself and establish boundaries. Don't ignore red flags. Know who you are and what you're not going to allow, even from yourself and stand on it.

4. Always have emergency cash or an account that your abuser doesn't know about.

5. Never rely solely on anyone. I don't care if I'm

married to a billionaire. His funding would not be my only source of survival. I've seen too many people stay in abusive situations because their spouse was the sole breadwinner, leaving them with nothing of their own, not even a skill or trade. I even witnessed one woman having to ask for money to buy deodorant and diapers, and he gave her a $20 bill. Financial control is abuse.

6. Learn a skill set that you can monetize at any given moment, i.e. cooking, cleaning, sewing, editing.

7. I will always advocate for formal education because that paper carries weight. Get as much education knowledge as your brain will absorb.

8. Not everyone can afford formal education, and not everyone wants to be in debt. To you, I say: read books, listen to audios, watch Ted Talks and YouTube, and sign up for free or low-cost seminars. There are countless ways to educate yourself without breaking the bank.

9. Heal and love yourself properly so you can love others properly.

I have told you all this so that you may have peace in me. Here on earth you will have many trials and sorrows. But take heart, because I have overcome the world. **(John 16:33)**

Chapter Two

Get your credit up and your debt down

Cash is King, but good credit can get you things you don't have all the money for, or you don't want to deplete your savings on a big purchase.

When I first started purchasing nice cars, people would automatically assume that I had a lot of money. Back then, I would say I didn't have a lot of cash, but I had A-plus credit. It wasn't always that way. Going through my divorce, the proceedings lingered longer than I liked. My attorney wanted to ensure that I parted ways with only the debts that I acquired, which meant there would be another court date to attend. I said no. I'll take all of the debt, his and mine. Just have the judge grant me my divorce PLEASE, and it was granted.

At the time, I was young in my career and wasn't making much money—far less than the amount I used in the budget example you'll see. I wasn't just living paycheck to paycheck; that would've been a luxury. Instead, I was getting payday loans with high-interest rates. I learned when I could write a check to Walmart, the base Commissary, Domino's Pizza, and the gas station on base to where they wouldn't clear until after payday, which means I was spending money I hadn't received yet and put myself in a deeper hole. I wasn't enjoying life because I was only working to pay bills. Then it happened; everyone stopped accepting checks, and the base even stopped troops from dealing with payday loan companies because they were ripping us off with those high-interest rates. I needed a new strategy, and I needed it quick.

God gave me a strategy that I still use to this day, with a few tweaks over the years, of course. However, the concept remains the same: know where every dollar is going, pay off your debts, and avoid accumulating any new ones. I became debt-free by sacrificing a lot and living on a budget.

Budgeting allows you to see where your money is going and where you can possibly cut back. Writing out your budget is easy; it just takes discipline to stick with it. You budget, so you are never caught off guard by anything. If something small does come up on a whim, you'll have residual money to cover it. Constantly building your savings should cover the big things that come up, such as needing a new washing machine due to the other one malfunctioning. It enables you to save and splurge a little when you want to.

This was the strategy I used: I wrote my bills in a notebook, and I separated my bills by the 1st and 15th columns. Depending on the date a bill is due, I place the bill under one of those columns. Everyone's pay period is different. Those who get paid weekly can still create a bi-monthly budget. Please see the example.

Budget example:

June 1st

$1,500 paycheck deposit

June 15th

$1,500 paycheck deposit

June 1st	June 15th
-100 savings	-100 savings
-150 tithes/charities	-150 tithes/charities
-300 rent/split payment	-300 rent/split payment
-100 groceries for 2 weeks	-100 groceries for 2 weeks
-55 cell phone	-100 car gas for 2 weeks
-35 electric bill	-425 car note
-25 water bill	-150 debt payment for 12 months
-100 car gas for 2 weeks	-40 renters' insurance
-110 car insurance	-75 miscellaneous/entertainment for 2 weeks
-50 debt payment for 24 months	
-200 after school care for 1 month	
-75 miscellaneous/entertainment for 2 weeks	
$200.00	$160.00

Keep in mind that you'll be receiving pay raises, which will put more money back into your pockets, and as you pay your debts off, you'll be freeing up your money to add to other debts to get them paid off quicker. You can even add a little extra to your miscellaneous money.

If you work hard at this, you'll eventually get to play hard responsibly! It may take time to get to the point of playing hard. It took me 5 years to get out of debt, and I didn't get to have a miscellaneous/entertainment column in my budget, so be patient with the process. You'll see people vacationing and seemingly enjoying life, but you're sacrificing now so you can truly enjoy life without robbing Peter to pay Paul later.

Let's discuss a few different strategies to pay down your debts. First and foremost, pay all of your bills on time. This greatly boosts your credit score, showing creditors that you're financially mature. I called and negotiated with creditors; some allowed me to do a lump sum pay-off amount. Others lowered interest rates, etc. You can either pay the higher balances first or the lower balances. I paid the lower balances because I liked seeing zero balances quickly. It let me know that I was becoming financially free.

One effective debt reduction technique I recommend is the *"snowball effect."* This involves prioritizing the payment of your smallest debts first while maintaining minimum payments on larger ones. Once a debt is cleared, allocate the payment amount to the next debt's minimum until it's completely paid off. This creates the snowball effect, which occurs when you pay off one debt, freeing up more cash for the next. This approach can encourage you to stay on course and help you pay off debt more quickly.

Creditor	Amount Owed	Minimum Payment	Snowball Payment
Doctor Bill	$ 555	$ 100	paid in full
Car Dealer	$ 3,330	$ 250	$250+$100=$350
Airline Credit Card	$ 4,500	$ 300	$300+$350=$650
Student Loan	$ 82,000	$ 1,000	$1,000+$650=$1,650

Owe no man nothing but to love him. (**Romans 13:8**)

Chapter Three

Second Chances

During my retirement from the military farewell speech, I shared how, in my 21-year career, I only had one regret and thought that was a good track record for that timeframe. I didn't mention how, in 2012, I attended a Prayer Breakfast at The Pentagon, where I heard the head Air Force Chaplain deliver the keynote address. He was responsible for every Air Force Chaplain, and as he spoke, I whispered to myself, "God, I want to do that." At that moment, I had never considered becoming a Chaplain; I didn't even know it was a career field.

I couldn't wait to get back to my office to research the chaplaincy requirements. I first stopped by my supervisor, Je'Nae Campbell's office and told her what I wanted to do. She said, "Technical Sergeant Haywood, I think that's a great idea." She was very supportive and always encouraging. I put my Chaplain Commissioning package together, which required me to get accepted into an accrediting university for a Master's in Divinity degree with a minor in Chaplaincy. I applied and was accepted into Liberty and Howard University. They needed my military career record, including but not limited to my physical fitness tests and annual enlisted performance reports. I also needed to reach out to some previous leaders for their endorsements. I had no problem doing this because I had learned as a young Airman to never burn bridges. So, everyone gladly wrote me a character and reference letter.

When I was a young sergeant, I had asked an Air Force Dentist (Colonel) on the eve of his retirement if he had any words of wisdom to pass along as I continued on my journey in hopes of retiring like him one day. He said to never burn bridges because you never know when you'll have to cross them again. He said something along the lines of people being unpleasant and flat-out difficult to work with, but don't burn bridges with them. This is a small world with an even smaller military; you will need those people again (emphasis mine). Those words stuck with me for the remainder of my career. I only burned bridges that needed gasoline set to them due to immoral, unethical, and unjust issues.

Once I had gotten my package together, I sent it to Captain Campbell, who then elevated it to the commander for his approval. During the waiting period, the enemy was working me overtime. He was in my ear, telling me I was unworthy of such a position. He said I wasn't smart enough and that I would fail. During this time, I loved God very much, and though I walked and spoke with confidence, I still struggled with imposter syndrome. It took my commander a week to approve my package, but the enemy had me trembling in my combat boots by this time. I'm saying the enemy because now I know that's who it was; back then, this was all me, and the thoughts were very real.

Everyone was cheering me on; my husband supported me 100% and was ready to make that move with his wife. My unit backed me from the bottom to the top, and I collaborated with the Chaplain who assisted me with the in-processing into their unit at Fort Jackson. Eventually, fear overtook me, and I found myself saying, "I can't do it." I spoke to my husband and expressed that I wasn't going to pursue it. I didn't admit to being scared; instead, I blamed it on money because, during the 3-year program, I would be demoted in pay to a Staff Sergeant. However, once I finished the program, I would've been commissioned as a Second Lieutenant. My husband wasn't concerned about the money at all. When that reasoning didn't work, I resorted to saying that I didn't want to owe the Air Force any additional time.

Listen, the Air Force never told me I would owe them anything. This was a bold-faced and fearful lie. Finally, Jesse said, "Kasha, do what you want. It's your career. I'm going to support you regardless." So, I wrote my commander an email expressing gratitude for the opportunity but stating that I was going to decline due to not wanting to displace my family and affect our finances. The commander called me and said, "Sergeant Haywood, this is a great opportunity, and I believe you should take it." Once again, I declined, and my career and life shifted drastically. I still had a successful career, but I toiled to the end. I ran into so many obstacles. I overcame them all, but they drained me mentally. I didn't understand how I had such a successful, smooth-sailing career to having to fight for everything. I remember being stationed somewhere and being placed with a supervisor who didn't like my face. She didn't want to breathe the same air I breathed. We didn't know one another, but it was so evident that she had something against me because a Lieutenant Colonel asked me if she and I had ever been stationed together. He thought we may have had a run-in at a previous base. I told him I'd never seen that Major before until being stationed here. That was another demonic attack.

I made my way through that period as well, but it nearly broke me. I remember driving down the highway and calling my husband, who was no longer living in the area. The Marine Corps had stationed him in another city. The secretary informed me that he was in a meeting and couldn't talk. Without hesitation, I dialed my friend and brother in Christ, Master Sergeant Anthony Bennett. As always, he answered my call with, "What's good, Hay-Good?" I usually laugh, but this time, I broke down and started crying. I was yelling that they were trying to break me! They're breaking me! He got me to calm down with some encouraging words and a prayer. After filing an Inspector General report and dousing the entire office with Holy Oil, God saw fit to promote me in the midst of chaos. I moved to a higher level of leadership and finally made it to retirement in sloth speed. I was emotionally drained, physically tired, weary, had a hard time remembering anything, and nearly spiritually defeated. My family had flown in the day before my retirement, and I didn't spend much time with them that night because I was tired and had to get up and go to work the next day. Yes, I worked on the day of my retirement. When I say I toiled to the end, that's no exaggeration. I was sitting at my desk, and when the clock struck 12:00 PM, I looked over at my Colonel and said, "Sir, it's noon." I'm going to start getting dressed for my retirement ceremony. He did the same since he was the officiator. After the ceremony, I met my family and friends back at our house. I spent as much time with them as I could. I sat on the couch for a while until I had to go to excuse myself for bed because I was tired.

I have now officially been retired for three years, and during a spiritual fast, God brought seminary up to me again; it's something he still desires me to do. I'm now in my third semester, and it's a lot of work, but it's manageable and very fulfilling. While doing homework one night, I said, "God, maybe I didn't miss it before. I know I wasn't this diligent with my studies back then." He said, "It would've been hard, but you would've gotten through it. Not only did I know the challenges ahead in your military career, and I was diverting you from that, but you relied on your reasoning and understanding and had to deal with the consequences of choosing your own way. That's why it's better to be obedient than to sacrifice." To this, I say thank God. He's a God of second chances, but I know from experience that it's best to trust his plans, not our own. I was in the wilderness for nine years because I was disobedient. How long will you be in there?

1. Is there anything God has told you to do that you're putting off for the right time or circumstance?
2. Are you afraid to step out on faith because you've failed at something previously, or are you comfortable with your current situation?
3. Maybe you're suffering from imposter syndrome, which is the feeling that you're not as competent and intelligent as others might believe you are, and you feel that eventually, people are going to find out the truth about you.

Spiritual warfare operates in the mind. The enemy plants thoughts. God did not create us to be divided against ourselves. As 2 Corinthians 10:5 teaches us, we are called to cast down arguments and every high thing that exalts itself against the knowledge of God, bringing every thought into captivity to the obedience of Christ.

To overcome these thoughts, I recommend sharing with a close friend or mentor that you're having them.

They should immediately build you up by telling you the truth of who you are. That's why it's important to have relationships where we sharpen one another. Then go into your bible and find scriptures about what God says about you, because all of those negative thoughts in your head are from the enemy, and they are meant to put fear in you so you won't obey God, but we counteract the enemy with the word of God. Here are a few scriptures to get you started:

- **Psalm 16:8:** I keep my eyes always on the Lord. With Him at my right hand, I will not be shaken.
- **2 Timothy 1:7:** For the Spirit God gave us does not make us timid, but gives us power, love and self-discipline.
- **Philippians 4:13:** I can do all things through Christ who strengthens me.
- **Isaiah 41:9:** I took you from the ends of the earth, from its farthest corners I called you. I said, You are my servant; I have chosen you and have not rejected you.
- **2 Corinthians 3:4-6:** Such confidence we have through Christ before God. Not that we are competent in ourselves to claim anything for ourselves, but our competence comes from God. He has made us competent as ministers of a new covenant—not of the letter but of the Spirit; for the letter kills, but the Spirit gives life.

- **Luke 14:27:** Peace I leave with you; my peace I give to you. Not as the world gives do I give to you. Let not your hearts be troubled, neither let them be afraid.
- **Deuteronomy 31:6:** Be strong and courageous. Do not fear or be in dread of them, for it is the Lord your God who goes with you. He will not leave you or forsake you.

Behold, to obey is better than sacrifice. (**1 Samuel 15:22**)

Chapter Four

Letting Go of Church Hurt

I was a pregnant teen the first time I experienced church hurt. That's when my pastor looked down at my stomach and stopped talking to me. We didn't speak again for a few years. My initial church experiences were full of judgment, rules, religion, and teachings about God always being mad at us. It's no wonder many people miss out on salvation at the appointed times because they feel as though their lives must be perfect before they can come to God. After all, man's religion has presented them with a God that seems impossible to reach and a religion that makes one feel unworthy and as if they can't measure up. Jesus already did the measuring up for us all. That's why God says come to him as you are.

I remember God telling me to ask this big-time drug dealer if he knew Jesus. He didn't tell me to condemn the man for selling drugs or to tell him that he was going to hell for doing so. He simply said to ask him if he knew Jesus. I was in my mid-twenties when God requested this of me, and it brought about confusion because it went against everything I had been taught by man. Yet here was God, himself speaking to me with concern for the drug dealer that he should despise and not care about according to man. What was I to do with this? So, I immediately started telling folks we got it wrong. God loves everyone; you don't have to be perfect to come to him. Oh boy, did religious folks come for me. They said I was leading people to hell with this message. Sadly, they couldn't wrap their heads around that type of Love. Let me not forget to mention that the drug dealer died a short time after God told me to reach out to him. Clearly, God knew he was leaving this earth and wanted his soul saved, but religion would've lost that soul because he wasn't righteous.

During this time, God was drawing me near to him. I had found a new church filled with some good people. This wasn't like the traditional Baptist church I had been raised in. It was so different that I didn't have to raise my pointer finger to walk out to be excused to use the bathroom. This had a different feel to it, but after being around for a while, I started to notice the flaws. There was the super religious crew that passed judgment if someone would take medications for a headache or received a diagnosis from a doctor. That means you didn't have enough faith in God for your healing. Then there were the "grown women clicks" that hung out all the time and ostracized certain women. I understand people can be friends with whomever they choose, but y'all know what I'm talking about. This was that catty middle school behavior done intentionally to make themselves feel bigger and better than some ladies. I must admit I was always invited into the fold, but I always gracefully declined because I've never been the clickish and follower type. I want everyone to feel included in organizations. Then, I witnessed the messiness where the pastor had so much influence on people's personal lives. If he told them to leave their mate, they would do it without questioning him. He had some level of influence over all of us. Yes, I was caught up in the mindset that whatever my pastor said was law, regardless of whether it wasn't completely biblically sound or not. It was revealed to me years later that this was an occult spirit operating in that church. That wasn't my biggest issue at the time. My biggest issue was that my husband was deployed, and we weren't communicating very often. I had a child with medical issues going on, and I still had my military duties that were a priority. I had a male friend, and we always bounced life's highs and lows off each other. During this time, I experienced more lows than highs, and he listened to them all. I found myself enjoying our conversations more and more. Before I knew it, I was longing for them, and suddenly, it became clear that this was a completely inappropriate relationship, not sexual, but emotionally. The Holy Spirit was convicting me, yet I found myself wrestling with my flesh. I wanted to cut this off but found out I couldn't do it alone. The situation and all of the emotions had become a stronghold for me. So, I scheduled an appointment for counseling with my first lady.

I found myself crying and being vulnerable, sharing all of my personal struggles with her. I was expecting her to say, "Well, sister Kasha, you need to fast for a week, and I'll do it with you," or "Sister Kasha, this is an issue of life, and I'm going to walk with you as you come out of this." Instead, she looked at me and said, "I can call the MPs (Military Police) on you right now because you are committing a crime. If I contact your unit, you would be in so much trouble." I was angrily thinking my First Lady was oddly threatening me. I was in total disbelief and in worse shape than before our counseling session initially started. I ended the session, and she had the nerve to ask to pray us out before we departed. It was as if she were checking a formality box. I was so confused as to why she would handle me like that. I was, again, seeing how church love and compassion weren't lining up with what I was reading in my bible and who I personally knew God to be. Eventually, I stopped talking to the guy, but that was just a bandage because I had not dealt with the root cause. It wasn't until much later, and I was more mature spiritually, that I realized that this was stemming from something in my bloodline, and I had to renounce it and deal with it in the spiritual realm. I found out that my first lady had dealt with me so harshly because her husband, the pastor, had been having an ongoing adulterous affair, and my seeking her help was actually triggering her. I came to three ungodly conclusions based on hurt: 1) I was never talking to church folks ever again, and 2) I have a conscience and a strong conviction, so it's just best I isolate myself and walk the straight and narrow path all the days of my life. This was a good one, but this was disconnecting from the community and leaving me with no accountability. 3) When I feel vulnerable about anything, have a trustworthy friend to confide in. I later changed this to have a spiritual sister that I could confide in. You need people in your corner who will lead you into truth with the word of God. Not someone who will advise you based on what they have seen on a reality TV show or read on some random blog. The wrong advice could have the Holy Spirit dragging you out of hell by my hair. That's something I jokingly say to women who share their intimate struggles with me. I tell them, "If you don't want to get dragged out of hell by your hair, keep your eyes on the Lord and sprint from all mess, because the Lord is coming to snatch his children up." That's how much he loves us, but when God disciplines us, it's uncomfortable and sometimes embarrassing. I say the hair thing jokingly, but it's not that simple. You can and will be set free from this. I HAVE FAITH IN YOU!

Years later, I had a dream that I was hanging out with my Middle Eastern friend, and she wanted me to wear a hijab. This Muslim crowd approached me, and this guy started yelling at me and saying I was being disrespectful by not wearing the hijab correctly. I was wearing it correctly. The issue was he didn't want me wearing it all. So, I started screaming and chasing him. My friend grabbed me, and she asked why I responded so erratically. I was consumed with so much pain in my heart that I felt it in my sleep, and I was crying and telling her that she didn't know what it was like to be born and raised as a black woman in America. I awakened and sat up in my bed, still feeling that pain in my chest. I began to walk in the dark towards my bathroom, and God said, "Kasha, you know that pain you're experiencing." He said, "That's how you are with my church, and it grieves me." God said to me that I was operating with the same spirit that a racist does when dealing with His church. The same way a racist would generalize an entire race because of the actions of a few, and I hate generalizations with a passion. Yet God revealed I had this same hardened heart towards the entire church because of the actions of a few. I didn't even realize it. I sat down dumbfounded for several minutes, repeating, "God, forgive me! God, forgive me!" Thankfully, He restored me immediately. We can't afford to be unforgiving towards anyone. It blocks our abundant living and prevents God from doing his best for us. I'm quite used to experiencing God's favor, but when I repented, more favor started to overflow into my life. My cup runneth over; the floodgates had completely opened up. Just days prior to this supernatural experience, I had prayed and asked God to reveal those things within me that I needed to heal from and work on. Those known and unknown to me, and God did just that.

Let's identify if you're holding on to church hurt:

1. Are you not focused on developing a relationship with God because you've felt judged at church?

Have you received snarky comments or eyerolls when visiting a church?

2. Do you feel like church folks haven't accepted you, or you've felt isolated?

3. I was hurt by_____

Let's heal from the hurt:

1. The church doesn't always go as planned in people's minds. People occasionally tend to idealize the church and struggle significantly to accept the fact that it doesn't always live up to their expectations.

2. Having people feel offended and hurt by the church is a tactic of the enemy, as well as having leaders in sin. Still, we, as the body of Christ, can overcome this setback by getting back to the bible, relying on the Holy Spirit and not ourselves, and having the best interest of our fellow brethren at heart.

3. Feel your emotions; sit with them for a moment because they are real and validated. Then, push forward.

4. Talk to God and ask him to heal your heart. You don't want unforgiveness or bitterness in your heart towards anyone. And remember, those who hurt you aren't God to you. This blocks your blessings regardless of whether you think

you're a good person. This will be a hang-up for God getting his best for you and a hindrance to your relationship with him.

5. Don't give up on church because you need community and fellowship. Don't allow the enemy to isolate you; that's when he attacks you the most. Take some time to find a church that aligns with your purpose and values to call home.

Two are better than one, Because they have a good reward for their labor. For if they fall, one will lift up his companion. But woe to him who is alone when he falls, For he has no one to help him up. (**Ecclesiastes 4:9-10**)

Chapter Five

Processing Grief

Grief can be a life-altering, debilitating process that makes you feel as if you want to join your loved ones in heaven right now. You're not necessarily suicidal, but there's a pain that takes your joy, appetite, will to move forward, and even your mind at times. I honestly didn't think I was going to survive the loss of my brother. My kids have always been my motivation to achieve more in life, but before them, there was my brother, Trumaine. Now, don't misunderstand me. I have other siblings, but my relationship with Trumaine was different. If you were to ask my siblings, they each had a different relationship with him as well.

He was the protector of the family, both young and old. I jokingly say that he would beat us all up, but he wasn't going to allow anyone else to touch us. He was the little big brother, and he was well respected by his family and his community. Trumaine was filled with wisdom, and intelligence that I know came from God. However, he struggled in this world from being a black little boy with a target on his back by the enemy. There is a demonic target on the backs of black men and if you look around, it's quite evident. Everything isn't about race, but I will not be ignorant to the fact that racism in all of its forms: Interpersonal, Institutional, Structural and Internalized are all controlled by spiritual principalities of darkness. I have friends of all races and nationalities, and we have candid conversations often about injustices in this land. I mentioned all of this because my brother was a victim of this, and it ultimately took his life.

While making his funeral arrangements, I was sitting alone in the cold room at the funeral home. The staff member assisting me had walked away from her desk, and I looked at her computer and saw his picture. I recalled many of the conversations we had at that moment, and how God had been warning him through me, that the enemy was trying to take him out. As I looked at the picture, I found myself questioning God, wondering why I wasn't losing my mind at that moment. After all, this was my baby that I was making arrangements for.

Yes, he was my brother but, in a sense, my first child because he stayed under me like my child. When I spoke, he listened. When I said do, he did. When he wanted, I provided. I spoiled him rotten, even as an adult. So, I didn't understand why I wasn't rolling on the floor, under that table and screaming to the top of my lungs, or even hospitalized. I could not understand why I had so much strength at this time. Prior to this time, I had heard about this tangible love of God for years, and I wanted to experience it. I knew God loved me because the Bible told me, and I would have most of my prayers answered, etc., but I would hear people talk about feeling God's love.

So, I would pray that God would allow me to experience that feeling. I prayed this same prayer for a few years. Then I began to think people were faking because this was one of the most straightforward prayers I presented, so I figured it should've been answered quickly, but as I was sitting in this funeral home with a lot of racing thoughts, it happened. I experienced an overwhelming LOVE; I can't even describe it, but everything on the inside of me knew that God loved me. This love consumed my entire body. All I could do was say thank you, Jesus, and try to wrap my arms around myself in an attempt to hug this invisible presence.

I believe God waited for me to have that experience when he knew I would need it the most. I've shared with those closest to me that even in my darkest hours of battling PTSD and anxiety, my relationship with God and knowing of his love is what kept me grounded. I had no suicide attempts, though I did have ideations. I can honestly understand how a person without this knowledge of God can get to the point of no return because the enemy is weighing the individual down mentally. It's likened to falling down on concrete, and every time you attempt to raise your head, the large foot of the biggest bully presses down on your neck to keep you down and submissive. BUT GOD said, "I got you Kasha. I've always had you. I'm your strength even at your weakest."

So, it was simply me being in God, and Him in me that was keeping me during this time. He said, "Yes, you're hurting, but didn't I answer your prayers and keep my promise to you?" My prayer had been that no one, i.e., the police, would harm my brother. He wasn't shot, killed, etc. He walked into a house, collapsed and never recovered, so even in that, I praise God. God had kept his promise that he would send a comforter to comfort me, and that promise is available to all who accept it during their time of grief.

Ironically, I had so much comfort and strength that as I was leaving the funeral home, I said to my husband that if I could bury Trumaine, I knew that I could bury my parents. Trumaine's funeral was in May 2020; 18 months later, in December of 2021, I sat at that same table in that same funeral home and made arrangements for my stepfather, and 10 months after my stepfather, in October of 2022, I sat at that table again and made funeral arrangements for my mother. Though a couple of my siblings were at the table with me at those times, most importantly, the Holy Spirit was also very present.

That debilitating pain is gone. I now laugh, travel, and enjoy life like I did in times before the grief. Though I miss my loved ones, I know we'll be united again. I pray that everyone places their trust and hope in God and opens themselves to experience God's comfort, healing, and tangible love.

Grieving is a very personal process. The degree to which the loss affected you, your faith, your personality and coping mechanisms, and your life experience all influence how you grieve. The grieving process inevitably takes time. Grieving has no "normal" timeframe; it occurs gradually and cannot be rushed or forced. For some people, improvement occurs within weeks or months. Others have a grieving process that lasts for years. It's crucial to have patience with yourself and let the grieving process happen organically, regardless of how you are experiencing it.

1. Express your pain. You need to find a method to let go of the intense feelings that come with losing a loved one. It's difficult to think clearly during this period, so it's easier said than done.
2. Recognize that grieving can bring on a wide range of unanticipated feelings.
3. Recognize that your grief journey will be distinct to you.
4. Ask those who are close to you for assistance. Seek expert assistance if necessary.
5. Look after your bodily needs in order to support your emotional needs.

6. Watch out for warning indications of impending depression. If you become depressed, get help from a professional.
7. While some argue that there is no right or wrong way to grieve, there are undoubtedly unhealthy approaches, including substance addiction, excessive work, downplaying or ignoring emotions, and impulsive behaviors.

How are you coping with grief?

What are you struggling with the most?

In what ways can I assist you in your grief processing?

And the peace of God, which transcends all understanding, will guard your hearts and your minds in Christ Jesus. (**Philippians 4:7**)

Chapter Six

Breaking Generational Curses

In the military, we had to have annual physicals tracked by our unit to ensure everyone was in compliance and ultimately medically fit for war. In 2001, I went to my scheduled appointment, and the doctor was straight to the point. He said your breasts are too big for your frame. He asked, "Do you want to keep your military career?" I responded, "Yes." He said, "Well, I'm sending you to Saint Louis Hospital for a breast reduction." I didn't know what this procedure was; he didn't explain it to me. I don't know why I'm shocked because he didn't bother to ask me if I wanted the procedure. Nonetheless, I complied because I, too, felt that my breasts were too big.

In 2010, I heard the audible voice of God for the first time. He said, "No weapon formed against you will prosper." Later that year, he told me not to drink alcohol. I was confused by this because I didn't drink alcohol regularly. I maybe had three drinks a year, if that much. I would have one glass of champagne for New Year's, maybe a cocktail during my birthday dinner, and some spiked eggnog for Christmas. It was definitely not enough to be told not to drink. So, I began to self-reason with the conclusion that the message wasn't for me per se. It was because I had family members who struggled with alcoholism, so when I have my glass of champagne for New Year's, I shouldn't toast with them because God wanted me to be an example for them. It took me about an hour to come up with this conclusion.

It wasn't until 2015 that God said it again. He said I told you not to drink alcohol. It wasn't about the amount I was drinking; it was because there was a demonic spirit in my bloodline, killing my loved ones physically and spiritually. He said, I sent you here for a purpose, and you're on the right track. That demon was going to try to attach itself to you. God always knows the end from the beginning. I had become a wine club member with a popular restaurant at this time. One perk was receiving one or two exclusive bottles of wine every month. During this time, I was so stressed out from work, and I had a 2-hour commute both ways.

Once I arrived home from a hectic day, I would grab a bottle of wine from the wine cooler along with a nice wine glass, run a bubble bath, and soak in my garden tub while drinking the entire bottle. Then God spoke to my spirit again, saying, "I've always ordered your steps." He asked, "Do you remember when the doctor sent you to

Saint Louis for a breast reduction, and you were clueless about what was happening?" He said, "That was me." This pierced my soul the same way you wake up from a dream when you're about to fall. I jolted, and I started to cry uncontrollably because I felt I had disrespected, disobeyed, and dishonored my God, who had clearly been warning me and guiding my life. I had watched a few relatives battle breast cancer, and my cousin, whom I was close to in age, was battling breast cancer during this revelation. She later lost her battle only a day after her 41st birthday. I got out of that tub, poured those bottles out, and canceled my wine club membership the next day.

I'm not special; I know that God speaks to all of us in some form or fashion. I also know that he warns all of us about things that can harm and kill us. I understand there's a spiritual realm, and I live my life cognizant of both the spiritual and earthly realms. If you're living according to this world only, you're merely a puppet in Satan's playground. Turn your spiritual eyes and ears on ASAP. I have realized that many of the battles I've had to fight were passed down to me from previous generations. I don't want my kids, grandkids, or nieces and nephews constantly attacked in a realm they're unaware of, nor for sins they've never committed. I remember Satan trying to take me out as early as the age of four. I can still smell the stench of my older relative's breath to this day. Him sitting me on his lap in my nightgown, kissing me in my mouth, and asking me if I was going to be his wife. His molestation didn't stop that night. He went on to hurt other children as well. This was not the enemy's only way of attacking me in life; it's just the earliest memory I can recall. We've been battling for years, and God has declared me victorious in them all, but no one should have to engage in spiritual warfare that those before them could have dealt with.

This is why I worship and pray often, fast often, and sit at the feet of God, breaking curses off of my family. I pray for relatives who aren't even born yet and those I'll never meet in this lifetime, asking for protection to keep our bloodline free and to eliminate many of their battles. No one is exempt from spiritual warfare, but the next generation should not have to deal with their grandparent's demons. I even did a self-deliverance on myself. I had come to realize that there were things I was battling that had nothing to do with me.

I had prayed and fasted, but it just didn't seem to be enough. So, I did further research, and I knew this was spiritual warfare that had been passed along to me. I was determined to deal with it because I didn't want my kids or other family members to be bound by anything demonic, especially if they didn't know how to deal with it. So, the night before, I had already decided which prayer I was going to use for my deliverance. I went to bed and woke up the next morning, ready to obtain freedom for my family. So, I started by writing a list of everything I knew for myself, and those things that I knew plagued my family. I even recalled old stories I had heard at family gatherings, recognizing that Uncle Pete had dealt with a demon.

So, I wrote it on my paper. I began my prayer and renounced everything I had written on that paper. Again, I renounced things that I had never done or seen myself, but I knew my ancestors had. I renounced things such as murder, drug abuse, and pimping, just to name a few. Then I proceeded to the next step, which involved a different prayer. There were four steps in total. I completed them all, and although nothing physically happened, I had faith that deliverance had taken place.

I went on about my day, reading scriptures and engaging in other biblical readings. Later that evening, I started to feel nauseous and began experiencing dry heaving. I was lightheaded, and I knew something wasn't right. I quickly grabbed the trash can that was next to my desk and started vomiting in it. I was hot and sweaty, and I could barely stand up. I started trying to call my husband's name as loud as I could, but the louder I talked, the more my head hurt. I ended up on the floor; I think that was because I wanted to feel the coldness of the hardwood on my body because I was so hot. I felt so weak and faint. I breathed and screamed for my husband as loud as I could while continuing to vomit. He heard me this time and came downstairs. He asked, "What's wrong with you?" I really couldn't speak much. I simply replied that I wasn't feeling well and needed to lie down.

He got me to our bed. I pulled my shirt off because I was burning up, and I lay there repeating Jesus. I woke up the next morning in that same spot on top of the comforter. I felt so light and free that I knew that my body had been purged. I looked over at my husband and said, "Do you know what happened to me last night?" He said, "You got sick." I replied, "Babe, I did a self-deliverance on myself, and it worked." I recommend self-deliverance for anyone feeling like they're dealing with demonic influences.

<u>Self-Deliverance Process</u> (Pastor Stephanie Ike shared these steps on YouTube)

Self-deliverance is reserved for those who genuinely want to be freed. Freedom is the goal of deliverance.

Give thanks to God for sending Jesus into captivity so you would not have to be bound when you break free from the bonds that held you.

Step 1) Recognize and acknowledge the demonic problem. (This is not a time to be in denial or prideful)

Step 2) Repent from known and unknown sins. Repentance is turning away from the things that have kept you in bondage and turning to Jesus. A few examples of things to repent from are addictions, lust, rage, and lying. When you agree to repent, you must remove yourself from environments that will keep you in bondage, like cutting off certain friends that you drink with. Certain relationships were only in your life to sustain demonic activity, so those people can't move forward with you. Stop watching videos that cause you to lust, etc. Eliminate the habits that sustain the presence of that demonic influence

Step 3) Write down things you've done and even things your ancestors have done that could have opened the door to demonic influence in your life and bloodline.

Knowing who you are and with the authority given to you, instead of engaging in negotiations with evil. You give the bad spirits the order to depart using your language of authority! Because your authority comes from Jesus's name. Renounce everything from your list.

Renouncement is to come out of agreement with the things you did because you are no longer that person. Also, renounce the things that were done to you because you are no longer a victim. Pray and say, God, I renounce and speak everything you wrote down. Be sure to renounce unknown things as well. Confessing your sins and those of your ancestors to God. Say, God, any demonic covenant through my lineage, I renounce my bloodline from it in the name of Jesus.

Step 4) Pray, Holy Spirit, whatever function and activity that I have been operating under that is not of you, reveal it to me. The Holy Spirit will bring these things to mind, such as anger, pride, control, suicidal thoughts, etc., and then call it by its function. Release yourself from the functions and activities of those demons by commanding, not praying. For example, say YOU SPIRIT OF ANGER, I COMMAND YOU TO GET OUT! With authority, call out every function.

Don't be alarmed if you start spitting, vomiting, have the urge to use the bathroom, yawning or shaking, because that's a sign that the demonic spirit(s) is leaving your body and you're being set free. It's also likely that the demonic spirit's personality has been presenting itself as your own if you've been influenced by it. So you will likely notice a change in your personality after the deliverance.

Step 5) Replace what God has delivered you from. For example, if you watch porn every evening after dinner, and it causes you to call your ex for a fling. Stop watching the porn and maybe delete the ex's contact. Replace this post-dinner activity with journaling or working out. Replace it with something that's going to keep you out of bondage. I promise the enemy is going to try to come back when you're possibly weak, vulnerable or distracted. Luke 4:13 tells us the enemy is always looking for an opportune time. Stay alert and self-aware so the enemy doesn't regain control.

Step 6) Renew your mind. Romans 12:2 says, And do not be conformed to this world, but be transformed by the renewing of your mind, that you may prove what is that good and acceptable and perfect will of God. Therefore, you renew your mind by reading and keeping the word at the forefront of your mind.

Prayer of Salvation

Dear Lord Jesus, Thank you for dying on the cross for my sin. Please forgive me. Come into my life. I receive You as my Lord and Savior. Now, help me to live for you the rest of this life. In the name of Jesus, I pray. Amen!

So then as through one trespass there is condemnation for everyone, so also through one righteous act there is justification leading to life for everyone. (**Romans 5:18**)

Chapter Seven

Release Every Weight

My maternal grandmother gave birth to 12 children, and they all were tightly knit until tragedy struck and caused them to be separated. I don't know all the details, but I was told that in self-defense and on two separate occasions, my grandmother took the lives of two men. She didn't serve any time for the first life, but for the second, she was sentenced to serve a prison sentence. During this time, all 12 of her children were separated and placed into different foster homes. My mother, Deborah Alethea, was number 8 of her 12 siblings. During a general conversation, my aunt Barbara recently told me that they (all her siblings) left home for school; she was in the 2nd grade, so my mom was in 3rd grade. Aunt Barbra said some people came to their school and took them away. She told me it was just awful. She said, "Can you imagine leaving your house with all your brothers and sisters like you always do and never seeing them again for years." That broke my heart even more for my mother. I knew she had a rough upbringing, but she never expressed it to me the way my Aunt Barbra had done.

After speaking with Aunt Barbra, I went to the back bedroom where my mom, who had recently been released from the hospital into hospice care, was resting. I rubbed her hand, gave her head kisses, and put anointing oil on her from head to feet. I said, "Mi Madre," that's what I always lovingly called her. I said, "You held on to too much." What I meant by that was my mom had been diagnosed with multiple cancers, some I can't pronounce nor had I ever heard of. The most critical one, the doctor said, was that only 1% of the population had been diagnosed with that type of cancer. It was just that rare. The Holy Spirit revealed to me that my mother had so much pinned up on the inside of her that she had never released it, and it manifested into these different cancers.

My mother was spiritually strong and a woman of great faith; I'm talking about bible reading and prayers throughout her day, from the time she would rise in the morning until she went to bed at night. She was physically strong from working out nearly every day, so I couldn't understand how she could get so sick. Mom had years of unhealthy emotions and pinned up stress from various life circumstances and inflammation inside of her body. These things that needed to come out needed to be released in her. I know she didn't understand that because she would've done what was needed. I didn't even understand it until I received this divine revelation.

I don't ever want to see another person suffer like my mother did. I want people to heal from traumatic experiences in a healthy way. Avoiding thoughts and reminders of those experiences is a temporary bandage for your mind, but the toxicity from it is still affecting your cells, organs, and other body parts in the form of inflammation. Inflammation is something our body may experience on a daily basis. Pain, swelling, body discomfort, joint stiffness, and insomnia can be signs of inflammation.

If you don't heal and overcome negative experiences, they can manifest into diseases such as cancer, autoimmune disorders, fibromyalgia, cardiovascular issues, Alzheimer's, and asthma, just to name a few. You can do so by seeking spiritual counseling, working with a therapist, a holistic coach, or all of them combined. Yes, I too have had to release from multiple traumas. Release it, so you can live in the wholeness and purpose of your life.

Inflammation can also be caused by lifestyle risk factors such as drinking alcohol, using illegal drugs, some (not all) prescription medications, smoking, eating poorly, not moving your body enough, engaging in unhealthy sexual behavior, being overweight or underweight, working too much, and pollutants and chemicals in water, air, food and products. In addition to emotional, mental, and physical stress, bodies naturally utilize inflammation as a defense against various kinds of stressors. Your body may be secretly blazing with inflammation even though you cannot see it or feel it.

All hope is not lost. Inflammation can be reduced by changing and modifying your lifestyle. This will significantly improve overall health. Ways to reduce inflammation:

- o Include anti-inflammatory foods in your daily diet.
  - o Anti-Inflammatory Foods (non-exhaustive):
    - § Kale
    - § Turmeric
    - § Fresh Pineapple
    - § Broccoli
    - § Blueberries
    - § Raspberries
    - § Grapes
    - § Green Tea
    - § Matcha Tea
    - § Garlic
    - § Virgin Coconut Oil

- § Olive Oil
- § Oatmeal
- § Salmon
- § Almonds

o Attain a healthy body weight (this could potentially lessen or eliminate the need for prescription medications; consult your doctor).

o Stop drinking alcohol, smoking & and illicit drug use (get professional assistance if needed).

o Exercise three to five days a week for 30 minutes.

o Hydrate and flush toxins from your body with water daily.

List the weights you are carrying _____
_____
_____
_____
_____
_____
_____

Now, let's release them. Say Lord, I choose to forgive/release _____ for _____, which made me feel _____.

Lord, I choose not to hold on to _____. I thank you for setting me free from the bondage of _____. I ask you to heal my wounded emotions. I now ask you to bless those who have caused me pain. In Jesus' name, Amen.

Therefore, since we are surrounded by such a great cloud of witnesses, let us throw off everything that hinders and the sin that so easily entangles. And let us run with perseverance the race marked out for us. (**Hebrews 12:1**)

Chapter Eight

Leave a Legacy

It was August 22, 2022. I was sitting in my mother's den, and I called my sisters Tasha and Brandi to tell them I was about to type up mom's will. Mom was battling cancer, and though I didn't believe she was going to pass away, I was still feeling a sense of urgency to draft up a will for her. I had been traveling home once a month for over a year. When I wasn't there, one of my sisters or aunts would travel into town to look after her. We had a pretty good system going.

I would always bring work with me to keep my mind occupied from dealing with seeing her in chemo. This time, I said, rather than focusing on the government's work and tasks, I should focus on preserving my mom's legacy for our family. I found a template, and I proceeded with the family's business. I had watched my mom work hard over the years, and sometimes, she worked multiple jobs, not out of necessity, but because she had the energy and financial goals to do so. I remember her doubling and sometimes tripling her mortgage payment because she wanted her house paid off in seven years, and she did it.

I had heard horror stories about how people would pass away, and the state would end up taking their property because their affairs weren't in order. I said that would not happen to my family. Mom had worked too hard for someone to just take her property.

It took me about a day to complete because I didn't want to leave anything out. Plus, my mom used to tutor college English, so I made sure to review it multiple times for grammatical errors before giving it to her for her review and approval. I entered her room, raised her hospital bed and said Mom, it's done. I thought she might be too tired for a thorough review, but when she said, "Pass me my reading glasses." I knew she wasn't too tired. While trying not to cause her too much strain, I said, "Mom, I ensured everything is being left to your kids equally. You have always said you want things fair, and that's what I've done. She went line by line, asking questions and making suggestions. Once it was to her liking, I called the notary, and she came over and witnessed Mom sign her will.

I felt so accomplished doing my mom's will that I did other family members' wills for them and had them notarized the same day. My mother passed away on October 20, 2022. Less than two months after I finalized her will. Having the will has proven to have saved me and my siblings thousands of dollars. We avoided lots of court costs, and my lawyer is currently working on recreating the deeds to mom's property to my and my siblings' names. This was all accomplished because I took the time to create a will. Next, I'm working on an Estate Trust for all legacy properties to be placed in after all deeds have been recreated.

You also have to protect your family's property and estates from scammers and conniving relatives who take advantage of the elderly. My Uncle A.D. (My father's only brother) passed away at the age of 43 when I was only 6 years old. Thirty-five years later, in 2015, his son Alfred called me and said his sister, whom I'll refer to as Aye, had some documents that she illegally obtained from my father. My father was dealing with what we now know as the onset of Dementia, and she had him sign all types of documents giving her all of his assets, including his bank accounts, pensions, etc. She also had all of my deceased grandmother's assets tied into this. Aye had durable powers of attorneys and wills drafted up. She went so far as to steal everything from the family by ensuring that if something happened to her, everything she was illegally trying to take would go to her daughter. I personally had never seen her daughter a day in my life, and I hadn't even seen Aye since I was a young girl, maybe 5 or 6 years old. I'm wondering where this girl came from. I found out from her brother Alfred and one of her other siblings that she's a con artist, and she goes around preying on the elderly. She had successfully done this same scam to an uncle on their mother's side of the family. They told me she had taken that man's car and everything. I said, well, she got the right one now. She was able to pull this much of the scandal off with my dad by having a lawyer who has been a friend of hers since high school to notarize and file all of these documents for her within the legal system.

But be confident that God is in control of all things, at all times, and what the enemy intends for bad, God is always working behind the scenes to turn around for your good. If I never knew this before, God taught me at this time. I hadn't retired from the military yet, so I took leave to Georgia to find out what was going on. At the time, the city was renovating my dad's house. The house was found to be in a historical district, and the city wanted to preserve its historical structure. I was told that Aye had taken these documents to the company responsible for the project. I contacted the city hall, and I could tell the lady who answered the phone was a little older and of Caucasian descent. She began to weep when I told her who I was and why I was calling. She said that she had been praying and trying to find someone in my family for months besides my cousin. She said that she knew my cousin was up to no good and that she knew she was dealing with a case of elderly abuse. She said whenever she asked my father if he had kids or other relatives, my cousin would take over the conversation and say no, *"I'm all he has."* As this lady was telling me all of this, I honestly became extremely mad because my father wasn't neglected. I spoke to him on the phone a few times a week. I knew his memory wasn't as sharp as it used to be, but I looked at him as if he was aging. My father always had a good memory. He would tell certain facts by date, going all the way back to the 50s. He would say to me. *"Your mom was born January 23, 1956, and I was flying a kite when she was born." "I know this because that's the same day and time I was attending my cousin's funeral, and after the funeral, we flew kites."* Every story he would tell me about the world, he would always associate it with a date, and I loved that about our time spent together because I love history of any kind. During this time, he would start being off by a year or so. For example, he would say, *"Kasha, you were born in 1978,"* and I would correct him, saying, *"No, Daddy, it was 1979."* Again, he knew what he was talking about; just a little off with the date, so I only attributed it to Daddy getting old. I never thought of dementia. I was financially taking care of my father, just as I still do today. I ensured Meals on Wheels delivered meals to his home because I no longer wanted him to attempt to cook or worry about groceries. He was still driving and going around to see his family and friends, and the DMV had just renewed his license, so I really wasn't too concerned. The issue was that I was in the military and lived in Virginia, so I wasn't physically able to be there. But for Aye to come in and act like he had no family outside of her, as if his kids were nonexistent, angered me to the core of my soul. However, the still voice of God said, *"Don't be angry. Now you know what's going on, and you can do something about it."*

I asked this nice city lady if I could stop by and pick up the documents that my cousin had given her office. I was so anxious to see what Aye had done. The nice lady said she could only release the documents to my father. I told her to get the documents ready because I was going to pick up my father, and we would be there in less than an hour to get the documents.

Before going to City Hall, I stopped by the store and purchased a gift for the nice lady. It had touched my soul to know that someone who didn't know my father, but knew he was being mishandled, took the time to pray for a stranger and a situation that she could've easily dismissed as "Not My Problem." Her prayers allowed Alfred and me to be the answer to her prayers. When my father and I arrived, she sat us at a table in a conference room and placed the documents in his hand, and my father placed them into mine. I sat there for some time and read all these documents, with tears pouring down my face. This con artist family member had come in and practically stolen everything my grandmother and father had worked hard for in South Georgia; obtaining assets was not easy for black women during my grandmother's era, and Aye wanted it all and probably for the purpose of only selling it. It was of no sentimental value to her. She had no thoughts of legacy or respect for what her grandmother accomplished during her era.

I looked my father in his eyes, and I said, "Don't you ever sign anything anyone else gives you again. From now on, you need to call me before you sign anything, and I don't care if it's a family member." I asked if he understood what Aye had done. My father said, "I do now, but I didn't at the time." He explained that she did a lot of slick talking to him, making it sound like she was doing a good thing at the moment, but she was actually conning him out of everything, and he realized it. From the direction everything was headed in, I believe Aye was going to sell the house to the city as soon as the historical restoration and renovations were complete.

The nice lady referred me and my father to a lawyer who specialized in these matters. I called and made an appointment, and the lawyer met with us that same day. I had to pay the lawyer a lot of money to have documents revoked, redone and refiled by my father.

The lawyer gave my father the same speech and slight scolding I had given him only a few hours earlier. The only difference was that she included the fact that it was costing me, his daughter, a lot of money to clean up the mess. He understood and was very appreciative.

Dad and I had experienced a long day. After eating, I took him home to rest and assured him I would be back the next day. As I drove down the road to my mom's house, where I was staying, I couldn't help but find it a bit ironic. My mom and dad lived on the same street.

Literally walking distance from each other. Which was another reason I wasn't concerned about him. She would walk down there for exercise, and they would talk, and when she cooked her Sunday dinners, she always took him a plate.

I told my mom everything that had happened, and my mom gave me the backstory. She said that my Uncle AD's estranged wife had tried to brainwash those kids and told them that Uncle AD had paid for that house with the settlement money he had received from falling out of a hospital window while being a patient. She assumed he didn't give her a cut because of that, but both my mom and father confirmed that was a lie. They explained that Uncle AD did whatever he wanted with his money, and my grandma had already paid off her house while working for people over the years.

The next day, my cousin Helen called me because she knew I was in Valdosta because of a social media post I had made about there being no place like home. She urgently told me to get to the hospital because Alfred was on life support, and his wife was contemplating pulling the plug. I was in disbelief because I had been speaking to Alfred all week. I tried explaining to Helen that Alfred was fine; in fact, he was the reason for my trip to Valdosta, Georgia. As I walked around my mom's yard, the weight of the situation hit me, and I realized the profound truth: God knows all things and is truly in control, orchestrating the lives of those who allow Him to.

God had Alfred reach out to me a week prior, knowing he was being called home, but he had one more mission to accomplish: to preserve and ensure his grandmother's legacy would continue. Alfred didn't understand all of this; he was just letting me know his sister was up to no good. He didn't know the magnitude of what she had done. I called my father and told him what was going on with Alfred. He said he'd head to the hospital right away, and I assured him that I would join him there a bit later.

I eventually arrived at the hospital, and a lot of family was in the waiting room. The doctors allowed us to go to the back in twos to see Alfred and say our goodbyes. I initially declined to go back there, but then I thought I needed to see my cousin. I had to say thank you to him in person. I went back there, and he was on a ventilator, and his eyes were closed, but his spirit was still in his body. I'm not sure how I knew this, but I just did. I held his hand, told him that I loved him, and thanked him for his obedience in telling me what his sister had done. You know, whether it's right, wrong, or somewhere in between, a lot of people won't tell on their siblings, but he truly despised her character. I prayed for him and told him he could. When I returned to the waiting room where my father was, I saw that Aye had arrived and taken a seat beside him. Without hesitation, I sternly told her to get up. I knew then that I was a different type of angry with this girl. She got up and sat in a different location. The doctors came out and informed us all that Alfred had transitioned. I was so hurt. Everyone started to walk out into the parking lot, and my father and I talked and walked together. Aye walked over to the other side of my father and asked if he was okay, offering him a ride home. In my mind, I thought, "She's really pushing it tonight, trying to test me. Let me show her why she's not about to play with me." I stopped and spoke loudly and firmly, "No, he doesn't need a ride. He doesn't need anything from you. Can't you see I'm right here?" For the first time in probably 20 years, I wanted to hit somebody, not just anybody, but her. I could tell my daddy knew it because he got nervous. He said, "You're doing so good; you don't have much longer to go in the military. We all are so proud of you." Those words gave me a reality check. I had too much to lose, and people who don't have anything will cost you everything you've worked hard for. They are not worth it, so always walk away.

Protecting your family's assets starts by ensuring everyone with real property such as houses, land and valuable collections, including but not limited to art, precious metals and coins, have an updated will. A Power of Attorney doesn't serve as a will. Once a person passes away, the power of attorney granted to you ends. Ensure that your elderly or ill family members have a will in place. It's also a good idea to transfer deeds via a quick claim deed. A quick claim deed can be purchased from your local office supply store. The instructions are simple, but they must be legally notarized and filed at the courthouse by the person currently on the deed, along with the person to whom the property is being deeded. There is a cost associated with this process. The property should be deeded to the responsible person(s), and the owner was planning to leave the property in their will. I recommend this because even with a will, Property can still get caught up in probate court for years. People have lost property during the probate process and even passed away while waiting. This still causes the family to lose their assets. Above the will, I hold in higher regard getting a lawyer to set up a Real Estate Trust to put all of your houses and other real properties in it. This ensures that future generations will benefit from the properties. All of these things I've mentioned need to be discussed thoroughly with your family members sooner rather than later, and action must be taken before it's too late.

Please be prayerful and watchful of those sitting amongst you when making these decisions. Everyone won't have the best interest of the legacy of the family at heart. Listen actively, and if you hear someone too eager to sell property, against the rule of the majority, or if they are constantly looking out for their own self-interest, this is a good indicator to be watchful of this person. Again, pray, and you will be protected and led to do what's right.

A good person leaves an inheritance for their children's

children, but a sinner's wealth is stored up for the righteous. (**Proverbs 13:22**)

I wrote this book as a legacy to my children, grandchildren, and those of my bloodline for generations to come. I want them to pick this book up and see the many obstacles that the enemy threw at me personally and our family as a whole and see how God made me victorious over every obstacle, including those meant to kill me. I want future generations to understand that the enemy will bring about trials and form many weapons, but they do not have to prosper as long as you never give up. The fight will most times be challenging, but God has declared you victorious, so don't ever waver in your faith or lose hope. God has truly blessed my husband and me, and we want the next generation to carry on the legacy we've begun. Passing down built-upon wisdom and knowledge to the next, continuing to ensure that each generation leaves a legacy of God and assets for the generation following them.

I'm releasing this book to the public with the hope of inspiring and empowering women who can resonate with the challenges shared within its pages. I want these women to understand that they don't have to bear the burden of shame and feelings of defeat alone. Please know you can overcome the circumstances you've found yourself in, and even if you're no longer in those situations, you can heal and still live the best version of yourself. But whatever you do, don't let bitterness take root. I've found that the best revenge is to heal and boss up. Yes, you can survive domestic violence and divorce. Yes, you can get healthy and reinvent yourself, so you don't have to say a word when you show up because your presence speaks volumes. Eliminate that debt to enjoy more life experiences such as travel, fine dining, and exclusive entertainment. Be a high-figure income earner in the corporate world or as your own boss. Fall in love and marry your God ordained spouse. These things are possible; I'm here to coach you through them.

If you'd like more support and guidance on your healing journey and you're ready to level up yourself and your life, let's talk. I'd love to help you get to your next level. Click here to schedule a call.

Made in the USA
Middletown, DE
22 August 2024